I0617026

HEARTBREAK2HEALING

A 30-DAY GUIDE TO HEALING YOUR BROKEN HEART

It's time to heal, to open your heart again, to grow and to finally receive the love and life you've been longing for.

A LETTER TO MY DAUGHTERS: DESTYNI & DAKOTA

My beautiful daughters,

I pray that you discover your worth sooner rather than later; that you see yourselves through the eyes of someone who truly loves and values you. One day, the kind of love you deserve will find you, the kind that feels easy, safe, and simple.

Stay single until you meet someone who doesn't need to be taught how to love you - someone who already knows how to cherish, respect, and protect your heart. Wait for the one who listens when you speak, who makes you feel heard, valued, and appreciated every single day, not just when it is convenient.

Choose a partner who invests in your peace, your happiness, and your dreams. Be with someone who never stops showing you that you are a priority, not just an option. Marry a man who desires to be a good husband and not just someone who wants the title of having a wife.

Always remember, broken people break people, and hurt people hurt people. Protect your heart from those who lack empathy and cannot truly love because they are still battling their own demons. You deserve consistency. You deserve effort. You deserve love that is intentional.

Please, my loves, never mistake a man's return for love. A man who truly loves you won't put you in a position where you must question his feelings. Sometimes, they come back not because they love you, but because they love the power they think they have over you, knowing you will take them back.

You are worth more than second chances with someone who never valued you the first time. Don't ever settle for less. You are worthy of the kind of love that stays, grows, and chooses you every single day.

With all my love,

Mommy

Contents

	Page
Why is Healing Necessary	1
Introduction	3
My Story	4
My Healing Journey	10
Welcome to Your Healing Journey	19
Day 1 - Healing Through Acceptance and Reprogramming	20
Day 2 - The Power of Forgiveness: Freeing Yourself to Move On	24
Day 3 - Letting Go & The Power of No Contact	27
Day 4 – Healing Childhood Wounds: You Deserve to Be Chosen	31
Day 5 – Scriptures & Prayer: Healing Your Heart Through Faith	35
Day 6 – Affirmations for Healing Heartbreak	39
Day 7 – Gratitude: Shifting Your Focus, Healing Your Heart	41
Day 8 – Self-Care: Choosing Yourself Every Single Day	44
Day 9 – Identifying and Healing Attachment Styles	47
Day 10 – How Are You? A Self-Check-in	51
Day 11 – Grieving Somone Still Alive	54
Day 12 – Therapy is a Tool, Not a Weakness	58
Day 13 – Take Your Power Back	60
Day 14 – Don't Lose Yourself: Be Patient and Kind to Yourself	63
Day 15 – Live in the Moment: Find Peace in the Simple Things	66
Day 16 – Meditation: Quiet Your Mind, Heal Your Heart	69
Day 17 – Trust the Process: Your Healing is Unfolding	72
Day 18 – Surround Yourself with People Who Love You	75
Day 19 – Break Unhealthy Habits: Protect Your Peace and Energy	77
Day 20 – How Are You? Check in With Yourself	80
Day 21 – Ignore the Smear Campaign	83
Day 22 – It's Not a Loss, It's Alignment	86

	Page
Day 23 – You Are Enough	88
Day 24 – Self Discovery and Personal Development	90
Day 25 – Set Boundaries: Not Everyone Deserves Access to You	93
Day 26 – Set Goals: Focus on Your Future	95
Day 27 – Make a List of Reasons Why It Didn't Work	97
Day 28 – You Deserve Better	99
Day 29 – What Did You Learn From This Experience?	102
Day 30 – Straighten Your Crown and Remember Who You Are!	105
Healing Exercise: Reclaiming Your Power and Self-Love	107

Why Healing is Necessary

Healing is not just about getting over the pain, it is about transforming it. If left unresolved, heartbreak can create a lifetime of trauma, insecurities, trust issues, and feelings of unworthiness. You begin questioning your value, your judgment, and your ability to love or be loved. That's why healing is necessary, for your peace, your future, and your freedom.

Bad chapters do not define your story. They are simply parts of it. The most painful moments can lead to the most powerful growth. Healing forces you to reflect, not just on what happened to you, but also on your own patterns, faults, and toxic behaviors that may have played a role. This self-awareness is where true transformation begins.

You know deep in your soul when it's time to let go, when it's time to move forward, to change, and to want better for yourself. Ignoring that feeling keeps you stuck, but choosing to heal allows you to stop carrying the pain of what hurts you. Otherwise, you will unintentionally bleed on people who never cut you.

Healing teaches you the power of releasing bitterness, especially in situations you cannot control. It helps you see that not everything was meant to break you. Some things were meant to build you.

"Heal so you can discover the happiness of wholeness."
~ Kayil York

The moment you stop living in survival mode and start healing, you will crave honesty, authenticity, and peace. That's because healing is freedom from your past, freedom from pain, and freedom to create the life you truly deserve.

Healing is necessary because **you** are necessary, whole, healed, and at peace.

INTRODUCTION

Sharing my story is not about placing blame or casting judgment. It is about truth, healing, and self-discovery. My journey has been one of pain, growth, and transformation, and I believe that by opening up about my experiences, I can help others who may be walking a similar path.

This is not a story meant to shame or harm my ex in any way. In fact, I hold no resentment toward him. Instead, I see our relationship and its end as a necessary part of my evolution. Every challenge, heartbreak, and lesson I've faced has shaped me into the woman I am today. Through reflection, I have come to understand how my past wounds and attachment patterns influenced my choices. I have learned that healing begins with accountability, self-love, and the courage to let go of what no longer serves me.

I share my story not as a victim, but as someone who chose to rise above pain and embrace growth. My hope is that through my journey, others will find the strength to heal, reclaim their power, and step into the life they deserve.

MY STORY

In 2024, I endured the most profound heartbreak of my life, a divorce that was both inevitable and, in some ways, preventable. I was forced to close the chapter on a part of my life I once believed would last forever. When my ex asked for a divorce, I agreed. At the time, the decision seemed straightforward, almost rational, but when the divorce was finalized, reality struck me like a ton of bricks.

How did we get here? My heart pounded with anxiety as I grappled with the weight of it all. A quiet ache settled deep in my chest, suffocating me. The person I once believed was my forever, my soulmate, the man I once called my king was now just a memory. My heart was shattered, and the sadness was overwhelming. I loved him with everything in me. I loved him openly, fiercely, without reservation, and I wanted the world to know. I nurtured him, cherished him, and honored him. I never expected marriage to be effortless. I believed it should be worth it. When I faced uncertainty, I fought for us. When he faced uncertainty, he walked away.

Watching him put more effort into leaving than he ever had into listening, understanding, or making me feel valued was devastating. Our marriage could have been saved with a sincere apology, with changed behavior, with effort. But his silence left me with no closure, only intrusive thoughts, sleepless nights, and an exhaustion I couldn't shake. I was left to process it all alone, just as I had so many times before.

A Love That Once Was

When we met in 2018, our connection was electric, unexpected, unplanned, and undeniably magical. A long-distance love that ignited instantly. We talked for hours, starting each morning on the phone and spending our workdays listening to each other breathe when words weren't necessary. He gave me the time and attention I had always longed for. Our conversations were endless, filled with dreams, plans, and promises. I was an open book (as he would say), eager to share my life with him. I created a safe space for him, a sanctuary of peace and acceptance.

When he moved in with me in late 2019, I realized almost immediately that the man I had fallen in love with was not the same man who now shared my home. The warmth of his words faded into silence. The affection that once came so easily disappeared. The effortless connection we had was gone. Quality time became non-existent. I found myself grasping for the love that once felt so secure.

He withdrew into himself, immersing his time in politics, sports, get-rich-quick schemes, everything but me. His friends and family got the excitement, the laughter, the conversations I craved. I felt like an outsider, a stranger to the man I once believed would be my lifelong partner. Everything I had fallen for had vanished.

I'm naturally affectionate, so I tried to maintain the connection in small ways, randomly touching him, sneaking a playful caress while he cooked or walked by, I was always met with rejection. He would push my hand away as if I were an intrusion. I was crushed. The love of my life was indirectly telling me that my gestures were unwelcome. Soon after, I received a lecture on "personal space." When I stopped, he didn't seem to mind. I respected his boundaries, but deep inside, I never felt more unwanted, unappreciated, or unloved. While I was building bridges, he was building walls.

When I voiced my concerns about how his actions were affecting me, I was met with silence or dismissed with a simple, "I'm processing it," leaving me to cope with my emotions alone. There was never a resolution, only an ever-growing chasm between us. The man who once prioritized me now treated me as an afterthought. Yet, despite all the red flags, I held onto hope. I clung to broken promises, convincing myself that the man I fell in love with would return. I wanted him to see me again - the woman who cooked for him, served him, and introduced him to new experiences; the woman he once called his queen.

The Beginning of the End

By 2021, I couldn't take it anymore. I suggested a separation, hoping he would fight for us. Instead, he agreed without hesitation and moved back to his hometown. I was hurt. I wanted him to choose me, but he didn't.

The pain was unbearable. One night, overwhelmed by my emotions, I left my children with family and got in my car, driving aimlessly south from Atlanta. I found myself in Florida, caught in a torrential downpour, unaware that I had driven straight into areas under tornado warnings. I checked into a hotel in Gainesville, unable to eat, unable to sleep, only able to cry. Seeking help, I called my doctor and was prescribed medication for depression. Still, no pill could numb the love I still held for him.

Despite everything, I reached out to him, and he was willing to rekindle what was left. We slipped back into our long-distance rhythm: calls, morning check-ins, and late-night whispers. This time, we decided that if we were going to make it work, we should get married first. Surely, marriage would make him choose me, right?

A Vow and a Realization

In September 2021, we married in a small ceremony in Folly Beach, SC. I paid for and planned every detail with hope in my heart. For a moment, it seemed like things were finally falling into place, but within months, the reality of who he was resurfaced, the same coldness, the same emotional distance, the same neglect. I found myself repeating the same pleas:

- What about me?
- I never ask for anything more than your time and attention.
- Our lives are running parallel, not together.
- I miss the person I fell in love with.
- I shouldn't feel this lonely when I have you right here.
- We don't spend quality time together.

He never heard me. He even forgot our first anniversary, another knife to the heart. I bent my boundaries, compromised, and discarded my own needs for the sake of love, only to realize he was never going to reciprocate. He was never going to make me a priority. He didn't value me.

I was drained mentally, emotionally, and physically. His silence only confirmed what I had already come to realize. My disappointment turned into hurt; my hurt slowly turned into anger; and my anger into rage.

To distract myself from the emotional weight I was carrying, I became preoccupied with social media. I found myself endlessly scrolling and posting, sometimes hundreds of times a week to take my mind off my reality. It became a temporary escape from the silence, the distance, and the pain I was struggling to process. So, I withdrew, seeking solace in renovating my childhood home in South Carolina. I stopped fighting for a place in his heart that had never truly opened for me. I stopped initiating conversations. I stopped asking for date nights, time and attention. I spent more time away, foolishly hoping my absence would make him miss me, but he was content. He had been emotionally unavailable for years. My distance didn't faze him.

The Final Goodbye

By 2023, we separated again. Just as before, the long-distance cycle began anew, but this time, I was in a different place mentally. My expectations had changed. There would be no moving back into my home. Whatever businesses he spent our entire relationship working on, he now had to make them work for us. If we were going to live together again, he had to secure a place for us. This time he had to prove his love with actions, not words.

While apart, he lived with a relative and later needed surgery on his shoulder. As his wife, I offered to come and be with him at the hospital, get an Airbnb to stay and help him recover, but he avoided responding. When I finally asked him outright if he was evading my offer because he was afraid that my presence would mean his relative wouldn't show up, his response was simple: "Yes." My heart ached because once again, he had shown me where I stood in his life.

That was the moment I knew. This would be the last time I allowed him to hurt me. Something in me shifted. I wasn't angry anymore. I was just… *done*.

I had spent years waiting for a love that would never come. I was deeply attached to the outcome, the vision of what I *thought* our relationship could be. I held onto the hope of a desired result, believing that if I just loved harder and sacrificed more, things would eventually fall into place. That attachment kept me stuck in a cycle of hope and disappointment. I had given everything, and he had taken it all without ever offering the same in return. I wasn't his priority. I never had been. That truth shattered me one final time, but this time, it also freed me.

Love should not be one-sided. Love should not leave you questioning your worth. Love should never make you feel invisible.

I let go. Not because I stopped loving him, but because I started loving myself more.

MY HEALING JOURNEY

After the divorce, I withdrew from everyone, including my family. I realized that I had spent my entire life saving others. Now it was time to save what was left of me. For so long, I put others first, giving, outpouring, and people-pleasing. I reached a point where I was no longer willing to let anyone or anything take precedence over my well-being. For once, I chose myself. I chose peace and success over replacement. I vowed that I would never again beg for someone's time and attention. Never again would I fight for anyone to choose me or see my worth whether family, friends, or lovers. This would be the last time anyone made me feel this way. I came to the realization that I was placed in people's lives to show them true love and loyalty, while they were placed in mine to teach me self-love.

This marked the beginning of my healing journey. I prayed and cried more than I ever had in my life. At times, it felt like I was dying inside. For months, I ruminated to the point of exhaustion, my mind was overwhelmed with endless "what ifs." The pain replayed in my head, deepening my suffering as I desperately tried to make sense of it all. Why couldn't one person pour into me the way I pour into everyone else? I attended a few therapy sessions, but the therapist I connected with wasn't the right fit. So, I turned to my faith and chose to heal on my own. There were childhood and relationship traumas I needed to revisit, forgive, and heal.

Confronting the Past

First, I learned that I had abandonment wounds. I grew up in a two-parent household. As a child, my mother and father were my world, my heartbeat. In fifth grade, I asked my dad if he would cry if I went to

New York for the summer to stay with my sister. He replied that I would have to wait until he left first. Not understanding, I asked where he was going. He answered, "To the graveyard." My heart skipped a beat. I immediately said, "No. Don't say that" and ended the conversation. Sadly, he passed away shortly after, and I left for my summer vacation to New York. Not long after that, my mother accepted a better-paying job in New York, a decision that left me moving from house to house with my siblings. From that moment on, I never had the opportunity to live with her again.

The abandoned, wounded inner child in me carried those scars into adulthood and sought the same kind of love I received from my father in every relationship - from high school to my last marriage. I mistook love bombing for true love, over-giving for worthiness, and developed a dangerously high tolerance for emotional neglect. I assumed that if I showered my partners with love and gifts, they would eventually reciprocate. I wanted to be loved, seen, and chosen so badly that I wasted time trying to make the pain and disappointment make sense. I tried to fix them or love them into loving me. Perhaps they did love me, but their actions proved otherwise, and actions cannot be misinterpreted or misunderstood.

The Truth About My Attachment Style

Through this journey, I discovered my Anxious Attachment Style. Anxious attachment is one of the three insecure attachment styles. Also referred to as anxious, ambivalent attachment in children. It typically stems from inconsistent or unresponsive caregiving. It is often characterized by low self-esteem, an intense fear of rejection or abandonment, and a tendency toward clinginess in relationships.

This made me deeply crave love and validation and struggle with a persistent fear of abandonment. This fear caused me to become overly dependent on my partners for reassurance, making them hyperaware of any perceived shifts in affection or attention. A delayed text response, a change in tone, or even a moment of silence triggered intense anxiety, leading me to question my partner's commitment.

Anxious attachment caused me to overanalyze my partner's words and actions, assuming the worst even when no real issue existed. My emotions tended to fluctuate based on how secure I felt at any given moment. When my partner was attentive, I felt a sense of euphoria, but when they pulled away, even briefly, I spiraled into doubt. This often resulted in clinginess, excessive people-pleasing, and tolerating mistreatment just to avoid being alone.

Healing from anxious attachment required self-awareness and a commitment to breaking unhealthy patterns. I have now learned self-worth outside of relationships, learned to self-soothe, and to communicate needs in a healthy way to cultivate a more secure attachment style.

The Power of Forgiveness

In prayer, I asked The Most High to reveal my faults in this relationship to me. Ironically, I was awakened in the middle of the night and heard His voice clearly: **"In order for you to heal properly, you must forgive him and apologize for your reactions to his lack of effort. Vengeance is mine, not yours."** I struggled with this, but I knew it was necessary.

So, I drafted the following email:

"I want to apologize for everything I've done wrong to you. I'm sorry for allowing my disappointment to turn into anger and my anger into rage. I'm sorry for all the times I excluded you. I'm sorry for all the times I was mean or nasty. I'm sorry for all of my impulsive actions. I'm sorry for not taking the time to pray with you "for us". I'm deeply sorry."

Once I hit "send," my anxiety instantly calmed, and I felt an overwhelming sense of peace.

A Harsh Reality

The Most High also revealed a hard but necessary truth: I had placed myself in this situation with my ex. I was the one who chose him and made him "my person." I initiated every major step in the relationship from defining our commitment, to moving in together, to marriage, and even the attempts at reconciliation after our separations. I introduced each of those conversations, hoping they would bring us closer and solidify our bond. In the process, I overlooked the still, small voice of The Most High, whispering that love shouldn't have to be forced.

I was pushing for something that wasn't divinely ordained and lost myself in the process. What made it even harder was that no one really knew what I was going through. I carried the weight of my pain in silence; holding my head high and always appearing happy and put together on the outside, while I was completely broken on the inside. I wore a smile to hide the sadness and kept moving forward like everything was fine, even when it wasn't. The Most High saw what others didn't, and in time, He began to peel back the layers so I could start to heal from the inside out.

Looking back, I now realize how deeply my **anxious attachment style** played a role in these choices. My fear of abandonment made me chase after an illusion of love instead of allowing it to come to me naturally. I was so desperate to feel secure that I ignored the signs of emotional unavailability, constantly trying to prove my worth and earn his commitment.

Although that realization was painful, it became an essential step in my healing process.

Stepping Into My Divine Purpose

While on this healing journey, I knew I was on the right path. I was stepping into my divine purpose. My vision became clear. I embraced isolation, realizing it was necessary for transformation and elevation. I had to surrender completely, releasing who I used to be and step into who The Most High was calling me to be. I had to break old mindsets, confront insecurities, and free myself from fears that held me back for too long. This was my pruning season. Everything and everyone that did not align with His plans for my life had to be removed.

This transition was uncomfortable at first because I was so accustomed to people-pleasing, but now I had no one to turn to but Him.

I knew in my heart that He was preparing me for greatness. My prayer life deepened. My faith strengthened. My pain was turning into purpose. Every day, I journaled and nourished my spirit with affirmations, scripture, positivity, patience, gratitude, forgiveness, and, most importantly, love for those who truly love me. My story was being rewritten. I was officially on the road to becoming *Queen V*.

Releasing with Love

While I forgive my ex, I will never forget some of his final words in his response to my email:

"I believed in you, and I believed in us. My bag. I'm sorry I gave myself up to you without judgment. Moving forward, I will only stay where I am appreciated and not just tolerated. I made you my world and my only option. I forgive you. Now I have to forgive myself."

Do I hate him? Absolutely not. I now see our separation as divine timing and divine intervention, something that needed to happen for my growth and healing. Is he a bad person? I don't believe so. Even though the relationship was marked by emotional distance and neglect, I can acknowledge that he had some good qualities. The truth is, he wasn't equipped to be the kind of partner I needed.

Contrary to my attachment style, he was a dismissive avoidant. This made it difficult for him to connect on a deeper level, and while I tried to bridge the gap, I eventually realized that love alone could not carry the weight of the relationship. Dismissive avoidants do not fight for love because they cannot handle the emotional intensity. Facing difficult truths, fear of being flawed, feeling unworthy of love, or confronting failures was too much. Shutting down or running away was easier than vulnerability and conflict resolution.

It is my prayer that he heals from his past traumas and realizes that despite those experiences, not every love is inconsistent or unreliable. I pray that he tears down the walls he has built around his heart and understand that he is worthy of love.

My final act of love was releasing him and giving him the space and freedom to go live the life he spent countless hours of our marriage planning for. I hope that my absence brings him the love and peace that my presence could not.

Had it not been for this experience, I may have never written this book or uncovered my true purpose. I wouldn't have found my passion for golf and hiking or learned to prioritize myself in ways I once neglected. While I am still a work in progress, I now fiercely protect my peace and energy. My focus is on what truly matters: my daughters, my well-being, my businesses, quiet mornings, and meaningful connections.

My story holds many more chapters, but for now, I will close it here.

To my forever person waiting to find me:

I've been through a lot and sometimes overthink, but I know that I am loyal, and my heart is pure. I don't give up unless I have no other choice. The only way to impress me is by being a good person. I don't care what you have, what you wear, where you live or what you drive. I have deep respect for people with pure hearts and good intentions. I still believe in loving and being faithful to one person. I refuse to allow this and other past experiences to dictate my future. I look forward to you understanding my story and protecting my heart and never allowing me to suffer the same pain again. I look forward to a stable and consistent love. I look forward to spending the rest of my life with you.

Lessons Learned:
- No matter how much you give, it will never be enough for someone who doesn't know how to receive it.
- Manipulation is when someone blames you for the way you reacted to their toxic behavior but never admits to the disrespect that triggered you in the first place.
- The biggest coward of a man is to awaken the love of a woman without the intention of loving her. ~ Bob Marley
- Loving a man at his lowest doesn't guarantee that you will have a place in his life when he's at his best.
- A man treats you how he feels about you. Once they show you who they are, believe them.
- Some people would rather walk away from you than face the reality of how they hurt you. They may choose denial over accountability and distance over honesty.
- Usually, the red flags you ignore in the beginning become the reason you leave in the end.
- The wrong man will find you in peace and leave you in pieces. The right man will find you in pieces and lead you to peace.
- There's a difference between a person who hurts you by making a mistake and a person who hurts you by continuing a pattern. Mistakes can be forgiven; Patterns should be broken.
- Love should feel safe and secure.
- The saddest goodbye is when you still want to hold on but letting go is what's best for you.
- A man will literally destroy a good woman then turn around and blame her for who he turned her into.

- Never regret anything that happened in your life. It cannot be changed, undone or forgotten. Take it as a lesson and move on.
- You cannot go back to the same well that made you sick just because you're thirsty.
- You can move on without closure and an apology.
- If someone creates distance between you, honor it.

WELCOME TO YOUR HEALING JOURNEY

First, let me say congratulations on choosing YOU and taking the brave step toward healing the most painful parts of your past. It takes strength, courage, and incredible resilience to face heartbreak head-on and make a conscious decision to heal. This journal is your safe space, a place where you are free to feel, reflect, release, and grow. Healing is not a linear process. There will be days that feel heavy and moments that feel light. Both are valid, and both are part of your journey.

Over the next 30 days, this guide is designed to help you process your emotions, rediscover your worth, and start rebuilding your life piece by piece, thought by thought, day by day. Inside, you will find affirmations, reflections, and prompts to help you reconnect with yourself, let go of what no longer serves you, and open your heart to new beginnings. Remember, healing takes time, effort, and patience. Be kind and gentle with yourself throughout this process. There is no rush, only progress.

You are not broken. You are becoming. May this journal serve as a reminder that you are worthy of love, peace, and happiness, starting with the love you give yourself. Welcome to your healing journey. You have already taken the first step, and that's choosing YOU.

Let's begin. ♡

Day 1

Healing Through Acceptance and Reprogramming

Healing doesn't happen overnight, and it doesn't happen without acceptance. One of the hardest truths you will face is understanding that to truly heal, you must accept that it is over. Whether it's a relationship, a friendship, or a chapter of your life, clinging to what was keeps you trapped in a cycle of pain. The moment you accept the ending is the moment you create space for healing to begin. Our minds often become our own worst enemies.

We replay moments, ignore red flags, and convince ourselves we meant more to someone than we truly did. This kind of thinking only deepens the hurt. Part of healing is reprogramming your mind and choosing to see things for what they were, not what you wanted them to be. Stop internalizing someone else's actions as a reflection of your worth. Their inability to value you does not diminish your value.

One of the most powerful lessons you will learn is knowing when to walk away, not to teach someone else a lesson, but because you have finally learned yours. Walking away is not about revenge, punishment, or pride. It is about protecting your peace, reclaiming your power, and choosing yourself. You cannot change the outcome of the past. What's done is done, but what you can change is what happens next.

You have control over your future, your mindset, and your healing. Every day, you have the choice to either stay stuck in what hurt you or take a step forward toward the life you deserve, and as hard as it may be, you must also accept that closure might never come the way you hoped.

Sometimes, closure is simply realizing that you are not meant to go back; you are meant to move forward. True healing comes from understanding that the answers you seek may never come from someone else. They come from within you.

Journal Prompts

1. What does acceptance mean to you in this season of your life?

_____

_____

_____

_____

_____

2. What are you still holding onto that is keeping you stuck?

_____

_____

_____

_____

_____

3. List the moments you ignored red flags. How does acknowledging them help you heal?

_____

_____

_____

_____

4. How has your mind created stories or "what ifs" about this person or situation?

_____

_____

_____

5. What would choosing yourself look like today?

6. How can you start reprogramming your mind to focus on healing instead of the past?

7. What do you need to forgive yourself for in order to move forward?

8. What does moving forward look and feel like for you?

Day 2

The Power of Forgiveness: Freeing Yourself to Move Forward

Forgiveness is one of the hardest yet most powerful steps in the healing journey, especially when it comes to forgiving yourself and your ex. It is natural to replay moments in your mind, questioning what you could have done differently or wishing for a better outcome, but the truth is, life is far too precious to waste waiting for someone to love you correctly.

You gave your best, loved deeply, and added value to someone who could not see it. That's a reflection of your heart, not their failure to recognize it. Forgiveness is not about excusing someone's behavior, nor does it mean granting them access back into your life. Forgiveness does not equal access. You can release the anger, resentment, and emotional weight without reopening the door to someone who was never meant to stay.

Holding onto grudges, replaying the hurt, or carrying emotional baggage keeps you tied to the past, robbing you of peace, clarity, and the freedom to move forward. Dr. Myles Munroe once said, "You preserve your peace by cultivating a mindset grounded in resilience and emotional intelligence." That begins with choosing to release what no longer serves you. Forgiveness is a powerful act of self-love. It is not for them; it is for you.

You did the best you could. You loved unconditionally. You supported, encouraged, and helped someone grow, even as they chose to walk in ego.

What happened to you was unfair, but staying stuck in that unfairness only extends the pain. It is time to forgive yourself for what you didn't know, for holding on too long, for loving someone who couldn't love you back the way you deserved. Say this to yourself:

"If I was ever the reason for someone else's pain, please heal them and forgive me. I forgive myself for every mistake I made while trying to love someone the best way I knew how."

Journal Prompts

1. Who or what am I still holding anger, resentment, or guilt toward?

_____

_____

_____

_____

2. How has holding onto this pain affected my mental and emotional peace?

_____

_____

_____

_____

3. What would forgiving myself and them free me to do or feel?

_____

_____

_____

_____

_____

4. What lessons did I learn from this experience that I can carry forward?

_____

_____

_____

_____

Day 3

Letting Go & The Power of No Contact

There comes a moment in your healing journey when you stop waiting for an apology, stop seeking closure, and stop begging the past to make sense. That moment is where your power begins. You do not walk away to teach anyone a lesson. You walk away because you've finally learned yours. You chose yourself. That is worth celebrating.

Let it end. Let it hurt. Let it heal. Let it go. Holding on only prolongs the pain. The truth is, to heal a wound, you have to stop touching it. Checking on him, rereading old messages, or scrolling through social media only keeps you trapped in a cycle of heartbreak and false hope. No contact is not a punishment, it's protection. Do not call. Do not text. Block him, his family, and mutual friends if needed.

Delete old messages and photos. Every reminder is a trigger, pulling you back into a story that is no longer meant for you. Close the door and do not look back. Cry if you need to. Cry as many times as it takes, but know, deep in your soul, that the door closing behind you cannot compare to the one that is waiting to open. Sometimes, the people we wanted most in our forever story were only meant to be a chapter. Let them stay there.

Let him go in peace because holding on to resentment, anger, or the idea of "what could have been" only keeps you stuck. You do not owe second chances to anyone who had access to you and abused it. There are better people out there, waiting for their first chance to love you right. Silence is your power. No subliminal social media posts. No reactions. No explaining your silence. You are not obligated to prove anything to anyone. Sometimes, the greatest revenge is simply removing your presence. Stop romanticizing what could have been. See it for what it was. The relationship wasn't lost. It was released. What's meant for you will never require you to shrink, beg, or break your boundaries.

Do not waste energy waiting for karma or obsessing over whether they regret losing you. Move on in silence. Letting go is strength, not weakness. You can love someone deeply and still choose yourself. You can cut someone off and still wish them peace. That is maturity. That is healing. Understand this: You cannot heal from someone you are still connected to. Staying tied to their energy keeps you from taking your power back.

Make no mistake, your power belongs to you, not to someone too arrogant or selfish to face the pain they caused. Not everyone gets a front-row seat in your life. Some seasons are meant to end. The people you once prayed to keep are sometimes the very ones you are better off without. Release them. Release the need for closure. Release the fantasy and watch how free you feel.

Journal Prompts

Write a letter to the person or situation you are releasing. Pour out everything you have been holding onto anger, love, hurt, confusion. Be honest and let your emotions flow freely. End your letter with: "I release you. I release the need for closure. I reclaim my peace, my power, and my energy." **Do not send it!** Instead, burn it, tear it into pieces, seal it in an envelope, or put it in your bible.

Then reflect:

1. What part of me is still holding on, and why?

_____

_____

_____

_____

_____

2. What does letting go create space for in my life?

_____

_____

_____

_____

_____

3. How does staying silent empower me instead of weakening me?

_____
_____
_____
_____
_____

Day 4

Healing Childhood Wounds:
You Deserve to Be Chosen

Healing doesn't just mean getting over a breakup or loss; it means going all the way back to where the pain first began. For many of us, that place is childhood. The version of you who learned to self-isolate, shut down, and bury your feelings didn't appear overnight. That version was created when you were left alone to deal with emotions no child should ever have to navigate on their own.

You self-isolate now because, back then, it felt safer to be alone. You learned early that expressing your feelings might get you ignored, dismissed, or worse - punished. So, you became your own comfort, your own protector, your own safe place, but survival mode is not living. It is time to break free. The hard truth is this - when someone truly values you, you never have to beg for time, attention, or love. They give it willingly, freely, because they want to.

Feeling the need to beg or prove your worth is a wound from childhood, a wound that whispers, "*I must earn love, or I won't receive it*, but that is a lie you no longer have to carry. You are no longer that child left to face the storm alone. You are grown now, and you have the power to heal what was never your fault to begin with. Healing means confronting those deep-rooted beliefs and rewriting the story you have carried for too long.

- Prepare to heal the wounds created in that season of your life.
- Prepare to stop isolating yourself when emotions feel overwhelming.
- Prepare to remind yourself that love is not earned by being perfect, small, or silent.
- Prepare to show up for the child in you who only ever wanted to feel seen, heard, and loved.

Journal Prompts

1. What childhood memories taught me that it is safer to be alone than to be vulnerable?

2. How have these old wounds shaped the way I connect with people today?

3. What would I say to my younger self if I could sit with them right now?

4. What does love look like when it is freely given and not earned?

Write a letter to your inner child:

"You did not deserve to be left alone with your feelings. You deserved comfort, love, and safety. I see you now, and I promise to protect you."

Day 5

Scripture & Prayer: Healing Your Heart Through Faith

Heartbreak may feel like the end, but it is often The Most High's way of redirecting you toward the love, peace, and purpose you truly deserve. There is healing in scripture, comfort in prayer, and restoration in divine timing. Sometimes, when The Most High shows you that someone isn't meant for you and you ignore the signs, He allows the pain to become unbearable until you have no choice but to walk away. That pain is protection.

That heartbreak is redirection. Trust that your heart will be restored, repaired, and replenished with an abundance of love.

Scriptures to Meditate On:

Joel 2:25 (NIV) – *"I will repay you for the years the locusts have eaten."*

Reminder: Everything you've lost, every tear you've cried, God will restore what was taken.

Psalm 112:7 (NIV) – *"They will have no fear of bad news; their hearts are steadfast, trusting in the Lord."*

Reminder: Keep your heart steady. You may feel broken now, but trust is your anchor.

Philippians 4:13 (NKJV) – *"I can do all things through Christ who strengthens me."*

Reminder: You will survive this. You will rise from this.

Ephesians 4:31-32 (NIV) – *"Get rid of all bitterness, rage, and anger... Be kind and compassionate to one another, forgiving each other, just as in Christ God forgave you."*

Reminder: Release what is weighing you down. Forgiveness is for you, not for them.

Proverbs 16:9 (NIV) – *"In their hearts, humans plan their course, but the Lord establishes their steps."*

Reminder: You had plans for love and forever, but trust that God's plans are greater.

Habakkuk 2:3 (NIV) – *"Though it lingers, wait for it; it will certainly come and will not delay."*

Reminder: Healing takes time, but restoration is promised.

Proverbs 16:3 (NIV) – *"Commit to the Lord whatever you do, and He will establish your plans."*

Reminder: Trust your healing, trust the process, and trust God's hand over your life.

Psalm 37:1-9 (NIV) – *"Do not fret because of those who are evil or be envious of those who do wrong... Delight in the Lord, and He will give you the desires of your heart."*

Reminder: Stop watching those who seem to be winning without you. Your blessings are coming.

Psalm 34:18 *"The Lord is near to those who have a broken heart, and He saves those who are broken in spirit."*

Reminder: You are never alone in your pain. Even in your deepest heartbreak, God is near, offering comfort, strength, and healing. Trust that He sees your tears, hears your prayers, and is guiding you toward restoration.

Prayer:

Heavenly Father,

I come to You with a broken heart, but I know You are the ultimate healer. Thank You for revealing what wasn't meant for me, even though it hurt. Teach me to trust Your will over my desires. Help me release bitterness, anger, and regret. Restore what was lost and fill the empty places in my heart with Your love, peace, and joy. Strengthen me in healing, guide me in growth, and lead me to a love that is truly meant for me. Amen!

Reflection:

Your heart is going to be restored, repaired, and replenished. The love you poured out will return to you in overflow. Trust God's promise. Your best days are ahead.

Day 6

Affirmations for Healing Your Heartbreak

1. I choose to accept that it's over and take control of my future.
2. I forgive myself and release the past—I am free.
3. I deserve peace, and I choose to protect my energy.
4. I am walking away because I've learned my lesson.
5. I release the need for closure and trust that healing will come.
6. I am grateful for everything that has led me to choose myself.
7. I love and care for myself deeply; healing starts with me.
8. I allow myself to feel every emotion. I am healing.
9. I trust the process—better days are coming.
10. I am worthy of genuine love, respect, and consistency.
11. I do not need to prove myself or defend my name—my peace is my priority.
12. I am not lost; I am evolving into my best self.
13. I release unhealthy habits and protect my peace.
14. I am enough, just as I am.
15. I prioritize myself, my growth, and my happiness.
16. I set boundaries because not everyone deserves access to me.
17. I am focused on my goals, and I deserve to reach them.
18. I have every reason to heal, and I choose not to look back.
19. I deserve better and refuse to settle for less.

20. Every experience teaches me a valuable lesson—I am learning and growing.

21. I straighten my crown because I am powerful, worthy, and resilient.

22. My heart will be restored, repaired, and replenished with love.

23. I trust God's plan for my life and know that everything is aligning for my highest good.

24. I am healing, I am growing, I am becoming the best version of myself.

Day 7

Gratitude: Shifting Your Focus, Healing Your Heart

Gratitude is one of the most powerful tools you have on your healing journey. It shifts your focus from what you've lost to what you've gained, from pain to purpose, from heartbreak to strength. Gratitude doesn't mean ignoring what hurts you; it means choosing to see the lessons in the experience. Gratitude is defined as a feeling of thankfulness and appreciation in response to something good happening.

But the real magic happens when you learn to be grateful not just for the good, but also for the challenges that force you to grow, heal, and choose yourself. Be grateful for the moments that broke you open. Be grateful for the closed doors, the unanswered calls, the people who walked away. Be grateful for everything that pushed you to stop settling and finally see your worth. *"I am grateful for my struggles because without them, I wouldn't know my strength"*.

When you look back, you will realize that every loss created space for something better. Every heartbreak brought you closer to yourself. Every ending made room for a new beginning. Gratitude transforms what once felt like defeat into fuel for your growth. The more you practice gratitude, the more you attract peace, abundance, and joy. Your energy shifts.

Your heart softens. Suddenly, you realize that what once felt like the worst thing that ever happened was really the turning point you didn't know you needed.

Journal Prompts

Take a moment today to write a list of things you are grateful for, big or small, past or present.

1. What struggles shaped you?

_____

_____

_____

_____

_____

2. What lessons did you learn from the people who hurt you?

_____

_____

_____

_____

_____

3. What simple joys bring you peace today?

_____

_____

_____

_____

_____

Read your list out loud and feel the shift in your energy as you remind yourself just how far you have come.

Day 8

Self-Care:
Choosing Yourself Every Single Day

At some point, life forces you to make a choice to either stay broken or rebuild yourself piece by piece. The most powerful decision you will ever make is choosing to fall in love with yourself the way you once wished someone else would. Self-care is not selfish. It is survival. It is healing. It is how you remind yourself every day that you are worthy of peace, love, and joy.

You are left with a choice to rebuild yourself, to find peace within, and to create the life you deserve. Choose yourself again and again. Fall in love with yourself first. Romanticize your life. Travel solo. Get in shape because it makes you feel strong, not to impress anyone. Make money. Learn something new. Discover what sets your soul on fire. Become the version of yourself, not for anyone else, but because you deserve it.

The truth is, when you start taking care of yourself, you start feeling better. You start looking better. You start attracting better. It all begins with you. Healing is not just about avoiding pain; it's about creating joy. It's about focusing your energy on positive thoughts, patience, self-belief, and self-love. You won't realize how much you've neglected yourself until you finally make yourself a priority again.

When you do, you will wonder why you ever allowed anything less. Choose to pursue and love yourself every single day. Fall in love with the quiet moments, the small wins, and the growth no one else sees. Focus on becoming the most healed, present, and whole version of yourself because the truth is, you are the love of your life.

Journal Prompts

1. What does taking care of myself truly look like right now?

_____

_____

_____

_____

_____

2. In what ways have I been neglecting my mind, body, or soul?

_____

_____

_____

_____

_____

3. What are three things I can start doing this week to show love to myself?

_____

_____

_____

_____

_____

4. What would change in my life if I treated myself like someone I was deeply in love with?

_____

_____

_____

Day 9

Identifying and Healing Attachment Styles

Attachment theory explores the psychological bonds we form in relationships, emphasizing how early connections with caregivers shape the way we interact with others throughout life. Our attachment style influences our sense of security, emotional regulation, and ability to maintain healthy relationships with friends, romantic partners, and even our own children.

Research identifies four primary attachment styles:

Secure Attachment

Individuals with a secure attachment style were raised by caregivers who consistently met their needs with warmth and reliability. This predictable environment fosters trust, emotional intelligence, and a strong sense of self-worth. As adults, they are comfortable with intimacy, able to set healthy boundaries, and openly communicate their needs. They do not fear rejection or abandonment, allowing them to engage in relationships with confidence and mutual respect.

Dismissive-Avoidant Attachment

This attachment style develops when caregivers are distant, emotionally unavailable, or dismissive of a child's needs. Over time, the child learns to suppress their emotions, assuming their needs will not be met. As adults, dismissive-avoidant individuals value independence to an extreme, avoiding emotional vulnerability to protect themselves from perceived weakness or rejection. They often struggle with trust, feel uncomfortable with closeness, and may dismiss or ignore their partner's emotional needs.

Anxious Attachment

Anxious attachment forms when a caregiver is inconsistent, sometimes attentive and nurturing, other times neglectful or unavailable. This unpredictability causes the child to become hyper-aware of their caregiver's actions, fearing abandonment and craving constant reassurance. In adulthood, these individuals experience intense emotions in relationships, often displaying jealousy, clinginess, or an excessive need for validation. Their deep fear of rejection can lead to codependency and insecurity, making it difficult for them to feel stable in romantic connections.

Fearful-Avoidant Attachment

This attachment style develops in response to caregivers who are aggressive, hostile, or unpredictable. The child grows up viewing relationships as both desirable and dangerous, struggling with trust and self-worth. As adults, they engage in a push-pull dynamic, wanting intimacy yet fearing vulnerability. They often struggle to regulate their emotions, distrust others, and may distance themselves from relationships to avoid getting hurt. Fearful-avoidant individuals experience both high anxiety and high avoidance, leading to confusion and instability in their connections.

Journal Prompts

1. Based on the information provided above, what is my attachment style?

_____

_____

_____

_____

_____

2. What patterns do I notice in my relationships that may be linked to my attachment style?

_____

_____

_____

_____

_____

3. How did my early experiences with caregivers shape the way I connect with others today?

_____

_____

_____

_____

4. What fears or insecurities arise when I think about intimacy and commitment?

_____

_____

_____

_____

5. What boundaries can I set to create healthier relationships moving forward?

_____

_____

_____

_____

6. What steps can I take today to heal and move toward a more secure attachment style?

_____

_____

_____

_____

_____

Day 10

How Are You?
A Self-Check-In

Take a deep breath. Right here, right now. Pause and ask yourself: **How are you, really? S**ome days feel light, hopeful, and full of progress. Other days feel heavy, messy, and impossible to navigate. That's okay. You are not failing; you are healing. It may hurt right now, and sometimes the pain feels unbearable, but breathe and remember that this too shall pass.

Everyone has bad days. Everyone struggles. You are not alone in this. What matters is that you don't give up on yourself. Pause. Rest. Reset. Restart. But never quit. You are allowed to fall apart sometimes, just make sure you always pick yourself back up and keep going.

Managing Intrusive Thoughts

The hardest moments are often the ones where your mind becomes your own worst enemy, intrusive thoughts creeping in, replaying memories you wish you could forget, questioning your worth, doubting your strength.

When those thoughts come, remind yourself: They are not facts. They are just thoughts. You do not have to believe everything your mind tells you. This is the time to keep your head high, even if it feels heavy. Remind yourself of your worth. Remember your value. You have always been enough, even on your worst days.

Honor What You Feel

It is okay to talk about what happened. It is okay to say it hurt you. You do not have to carry the weight of it in silence. Speaking your truth is part of healing. Never be ashamed of how deeply you loved someone, even if it didn't work out.

Loving someone fully is never a weakness, it's proof of your capacity to feel, to give, and to care. While it may not feel like it now, you are already stronger than you know. No one is cheering louder for you than the person you used to be. That version of you, the one who cried, who broke, who barely survived some days is so damn proud of how far you've come.

So, how are you, really? Check in with yourself. You don't have to be perfect. You just have to keep going.

Journal Prompts

1. How am I feeling today, physically, emotionally, and mentally?

_____

_____

_____

_____

2. What intrusive thoughts are taking up space in my mind right now? Are they true, or just fear?

_____

_____

_____

_____

3. What do I need right now? Rest, love, patience, or grace?

_____

_____

_____

_____

_____

Day 11

Grieving Someone Still Alive: Honor Your Emotions, Honor Your Healing

There is a unique kind of grief that comes with losing someone who is still alive. It is confusing, devastating, and often impossible to explain. How do you mourn someone who still exists, but no longer shows up for you in the way they once did? You will feel it all: anger, sadness, betrayal, guilt, longing, and a deep, aching loneliness.

You will feel like you have lost a part of your life, a piece of yourself, and the future you once dreamed of. That's because you have. It is heartbreaking when your favorite person, someone you built dreams with becomes just another lesson, another memory. You didn't just lose the relationship; you are grieving the life you thought you were creating together. The family, the legacy, the forever you imagined.

Give Yourself Permission to Grieve

You don't have to be strong all the time. Give yourself permission to cry, to scream, to break down. Grieve the way you need to. Grieve the version of that person you believed in, the one you sacrificed so much of yourself for. Grieve the best parts of the relationship you held onto, hoping things would get better. Grieve the future that will never happen, but also remind yourself that this wasn't all your fault. You cannot carry 100% of the blame for something that took two people to build and two people to break.

The Hard Truth About Healing

One day, you will stop crying in the shower. One day you will wake up and realize that you are tired of being angry. You will stop wondering what you could have done differently. You will stop replaying the pain over and over in your mind, and you will press play on your life because you will finally realize that you still have so much to live for.

It is normal to lose sleep, to lose your appetite, to lose focus. It is normal to feel guilty. You may even feel like you failed or let people down. You will be angry about not leaving sooner, for ignoring the red flags, for giving too many chances. You will ruminate, replaying moments that haunt you. You will wonder why it didn't work. You will wish it could have been different.

This Is All Part of the Process

Expect to feel an entire range of emotions sometimes in the same day, sometimes in the same hour. The highs will feel beautiful. The lows will feel unbearable. Unexpected waves of grief will hit when you least expect them. It is all part of the process.

Grief is not just about loss; it is about learning to live with the absence of something you once thought was permanent. Here is what you will learn: you were never truly dependent on them for your happiness. You are capable of rebuilding, of healing, of creating a new life, one where you come first. One day, the pain will loosen its grip. When it does, you will see that losing them wasn't the end, it was the beginning of coming home to yourself.

Journal Prompts

1. What parts of the relationship or future am I grieving most?

2. What emotions have I been avoiding because they're too painful to face?

3. What would I say to my past self who stayed, hoping things would change?

4. How can I begin to forgive myself for what I didn't know then?

Day 12

Therapy Is a Tool, Not a Weakness: Give Yourself Permission to Seek Help

Healing is hard. Some wounds run too deep to navigate alone and that's okay. There is strength in admitting that you need support. There is power in choosing to invest in your healing. If you find yourself stuck replaying the same memories, overwhelmed by emotions you cannot process, or struggling with anxiety, depression, or intrusive thoughts, therapy can help.

You do not have to carry this weight alone. Therapy is not about labeling yourself as broken; it is about giving yourself the space, tools, and guidance to heal properly. It is about learning to release what no longer serves you and making peace with what you cannot change. A good therapist creates a safe space where you can be vulnerable, honest, and unapologetically yourself.

A space where you do not have to justify why you stayed, why you're hurting, or why it's hard to move on. They will help you untangle the past, understand your triggers, and develop healthy coping skills to face life head-on. There is no shame in needing help. The bravest thing you can do for yourself is to decide that healing is non-negotiable and if therapy is part of that journey, embrace it fully.

Journal Prompts

1. What fears or beliefs do I have about seeking help or going to therapy?

_____

_____

_____

_____

2. What kind of support do I need right now (emotional, mental, spiritual)?

_____

_____

_____

_____

_____

3. How would my life change if I gave myself permission to heal fully?

_____

_____

_____

_____

_____

Day 13

Take Your Power Back

There comes a moment in your healing journey when you realize that it is time to take your power back. No more giving people, situations, or heartbreak the authority to control your emotions, your peace, or your future. You are not a victim of your circumstances; you are the creator of your next chapter.

Taking your power back means reclaiming your worth and refusing to let anyone's actions or lack of love define you. It means no longer begging for closure, validation, or love from someone who was never capable of giving it. You do not need their apology to heal, and you need your own permission to move forward. It is choosing to stop replaying the past in your mind.

To stop overthinking the what-ifs and maybes. What's done is done. You survived, and that alone proves your strength. Taking your power back is cutting ties with what drains you emotionally, mentally, and spiritually. It's standing tall, knowing that what was meant to break you only made you stronger. It's choosing yourself every single time. Remember: You are not too much.

You are not hard to love. You were simply trying to pour into people who didn't know what to do with someone like you. Your healing begins the moment you decide to stop allowing people who could not love you properly to have a front-row seat in your life. Protect your energy. Reclaim your peace. Take your power back.

Journal Prompts

1. What does taking your power back mean to you right now?

_____

_____

_____

_____

_____

2. In what ways did you give away your power during your relationship?

_____

_____

_____

_____

_____

3. What boundaries do you need to put in place to protect your peace moving forward?

_____

_____

_____

_____

_____

4. What is something you are ready to release today to reclaim your power?

_____

_____

_____

_____

_____

5. List five things you love about yourself that you forgot or stopped noticing during the relationship.

_____

_____

_____

_____

_____

_____

_____

_____

_____

_____

_____

_____

_____

_____

_____

_____

_____

_____

Day 14

Don't Lose Yourself: Be Patient and Kind to Yourself

One of the hardest parts of healing is realizing how much of yourself you lost while trying to hold onto someone who was never meant to stay. You may feel regret, shame, or anger. Regret for staying too long, shame for ignoring the red flags, or anger for believing in potential instead of reality. I need you to hear this: you did the best you could with what you knew at the time.

Please do not beat yourself up for the time you gave or the love you poured into someone who couldn't meet you where you were. That doesn't make you weak, it makes you human. You stayed because you had hope, because you believed in the good, because you wanted it to work. There is no shame in that. But now, you know better.

Now, you understand that knowing when to leave is just as important as knowing when to stay. That moment when you chose to walk away, when you chose yourself, that was your power returning. That was your soul reminding you that you deserve more, and you always have.

Be Patient with Your Process

Healing is not a race. Some days, you will feel strong and certain. On other days, the weight of the past may pull you down. Be patient with yourself. Talk to yourself like someone you love because you should be the first person you protect, nurture, and believe in.

This is not about punishing yourself for what you allowed, it is about learning from it. Growing through it. Becoming the version of yourself who will never settle for less again.

You Are Not Lost

You are still here. Still worthy. Still whole. You are not defined by who left or how long you stayed. You are defined by your decision to choose yourself no matter how long it takes.

Journal Prompts

1. What part of myself did I lose trying to hold onto this relationship?

_____

_____

_____

_____

_____

2. How can I show patience and kindness to myself today?

_____

_____

_____

_____

_____

3. What have I learned about my own strength through this experience?

_____

_____

_____

_____

_____

Day 15

Live in the Moment: Find Peace in the Simple Things

When your heart is broken, your mind often drifts to the past or worries about the future. You replay memories, question your worth, and wonder what's next. The true gift of healing comes when you learn to slow down and live in the moment - right here, right now. Start finding value in the little things, the moments that seem small but hold the most meaning.

Cherish your alone time. Sit with your thoughts, breathe deeply, and remind yourself that solitude doesn't mean loneliness, it means peace. Protect your sleep. Let it restore you. Take walks in the park and allow nature to remind you that life keeps moving and beauty still surrounds you. Feel the sun on your skin, the wind on your face, and the ground steady beneath your feet.

Spend quality time with people who love you and those who don't drain your energy but pour into your soul. Laugh with them. Cry if you need to. Let yourself be fully present in these moments, because they remind you: you are still here, still loved, still whole. Make simplicity your goal. Happiness doesn't always come from grand gestures or complicated plans.

It is found in the morning light, your favorite cup of coffee, a good book, or the quiet moments you spend with yourself. Healing doesn't happen overnight, but it does happen moment by moment. So slow down. Breathe. Be here.

Journal Prompts

1. What simple moments bring me peace right now?

_____

_____

_____

_____

_____

2. How can I practice being fully present each day?

_____

_____

_____

_____

_____

3. What little things have I been overlooking that truly make me happy?

_____

_____

_____

_____

_____

Day 16

Meditation:
Quiet Your Mind, Heal Your Heart

Heartbreak creates chaos in your mind; racing thoughts, constant overthinking, re-living conversations, and wondering "what if." It feels like your mind won't give you a moment's peace. This is where meditation becomes a powerful tool in your healing journey. Meditation isn't about silencing your emotions or pretending that you are okay.

It is about giving yourself a safe space to pause, breathe, and reconnect with your inner self beyond the pain, beyond the heartbreak. Even just 5 to 10 minutes a day can make a difference. Close your eyes, breathe deeply, and allow your mind to settle. In those moments of stillness, you give yourself permission to simply exist without judgment or expectations.

Guided meditations focused on heartbreak, healing, and self-love can help shift your focus from the past to the present. They remind you that, although your heart is hurting, you are still in control of your healing.

Benefits of Meditation While Healing from Heartbreak:

- Calms anxiety and intrusive thoughts.
- Brings awareness to your emotions without letting them control you. • Reconnects you with your body and breath.
- Helps release anger, sadness, and resentment.
- Creates space for gratitude, forgiveness, and peace.

Journal Prompts

1. How do I feel after sitting in silence or meditating for a few minutes?

_____
_____
_____
_____

2. How can I practice being fully present each day?

_____
_____
_____
_____
_____

3. What little things have I been overlooking that truly make me happy?

_____
_____
_____
_____
_____

Day 17

Trust the Process:
Your Healing is Unfolding

Healing from heartbreak isn't easy. Some days, you will feel like you are making progress; other days, it may seem like you are right back where you started, but no matter where you are on your journey, remind yourself daily: trust the process. Right now, the past might still feel heavy. The memories, the questions, and the pain may linger, but it won't always be this way.

Over time, the past will lose its power. What hurts today won't hurt forever. You won't always feel this stuck, this broken, or this lost. You may never fully understand why the relationship ended the way it did, but trust that its removal was a form of protection. Sometimes, losing what you thought you wanted is exactly what clears the way for what you truly deserve.

Not everyone is meant to stay, and not every love is meant to last, but every experience carries a lesson. Tough times are temporary. The heartbreak, the sleepless nights, the tears, the overthinking and none of it will define you. You are learning, growing, and becoming someone stronger, wiser, and more aligned with what you truly need.

Better days are coming. There will be moments when you smile again without forcing it. Mornings when your first thought isn't about them. One day, you will wake up and realize you survived what you once thought would break you. Trust the process. You are exactly where you're meant to be.

Journal Prompts

1. What am I learning about myself during this season of healing?

_____

_____

_____

_____

2. How can I remind myself to trust the process when the pain feels overwhelming?

_____

_____

_____

_____

_____

3. What am I looking forward to in my next chapter?

_____

_____

_____

_____

_____

Day 18

Surround Yourself with People Who Love You

One of the most important steps in healing from heartbreak is being mindful of who you allow into your space. After pouring so much love into the wrong person, it is time to surround yourself with people who truly care, those who choose you, uplift you, and remind you of your worth. Choose who chooses you. Love is never one-sided. Stop chasing those who make you feel like you are hard to love. You deserve to be in the company of people who never make you question your place in their life. Call those who call you. Visit those who visit you. Relationships, whether romantic, platonic, or familial should flow naturally, not be forced. Reciprocation is a form of love. Protect your energy by giving it to those who give it back.

Ignore those who ignore you. Stop watering dead plants. If someone shows you through their actions that you are no longer a priority, believe them. Their absence is making room for better connections meant for you. Go where you are celebrated, not just tolerated. Surround yourself with people who see your light, even when you feel dim, those who love you unconditionally, check on you without being asked, and remind you that you matter. Your healing journey is sacred. You need support, not people who add to your pain. Choose love that feels safe, consistent, and genuine because that's the love you deserve.

Journal Prompts

1. Who in my life makes me feel truly loved, safe, and valued?

_____

_____

_____

_____

_____

2. Who am I holding on to that no longer chooses me?

_____

_____

_____

_____

_____

3. How can I create space for healthier, more supportive relationships?

_____

_____

_____

_____

_____

Day 19

Break Unhealthy Habits: Protect Your Peace and Energy

Heartbreak has a way of pulling you toward unhealthy habits, searching for temporary relief from the pain, trying to fill the void someone else left behind, but the truth is, no number of distractions or unhealthy coping mechanisms will heal your heart. Only facing the pain, processing it, and choosing yourself will. You cannot fix someone who refuses to face or heal their own traumas.

Stop sacrificing your peace trying to save someone who won't save themselves. That is not your responsibility, and it never was. Protect your peace and energy at all costs. You are in a delicate season of healing, and anything or anyone that drains you has no place in your life right now. You have fought too hard to find this peace. Do not trade it for temporary comfort.

Remove yourself from unhealthy distractions. Scrolling through old messages, stalking social media, and replaying conversations in your head, none of it serves you. The more you engage with the past, the harder it is to move forward. Let it go. Do not stress over things you cannot control. You cannot control how they feel, what they do, or whether they ever regret losing you.

What you can control is how you choose to show up for yourself from this moment forward. Choose peace. Choose healing. No excessive drinking. Numbing the pain only delays the healing. You don't need another drink; you need clarity. You need your mind, body, and soul in alignment.

You deserve to wake up clear-headed, proud of yourself, and at peace. Healing is uncomfortable but so is staying stuck in cycles that keep breaking you. Choose differently. Break the habits that keep you tied to your pain.

Journal Prompts

1. What unhealthy habits have I developed while trying to cope with this heartbreak?

_____

_____

_____

_____

_____

2. What can I do today to break free from patterns that no longer serve me?

_____

_____

_____

_____

_____

3. How can I protect my peace moving forward?

_____

_____

_____

_____

_____

Day 20

How Are You? Check In with Yourself

You are not lost. You are simply in the middle of a transformation. You are standing in the space between who you used to be and the version of yourself that is still unfolding. Your old life, the dreams, the love, the plans are gone, but your new life, the one you are building, hasn't fully revealed itself yet. That is why it feels so uncomfortable. It's okay if you thought you were over it, only for the pain to hit you all over again. Healing is not a straight line. It is okay to fall apart, even after you thought you had it under control. That does not make you weak, it makes you human. Healing is messy.

There is no time limit, no finish line you must cross by a certain date. Some days, you will feel strong. Other days, you will barely hold it together. Both are part of the process. Be patient. Be gentle with yourself. Allow every emotion to pass through you without shame. One day, you will wake up and realize the heaviness you've carried - the pain, the heartbreak, the memories no longer weigh you down.

You won't know exactly when it happened, but it will. You will feel lighter, freer, and ready to live again. That day is coming. Someday, all the love you gave to the wrong person, the loyalty, the care, the effort will find its way back to you. It will come from someone who has been waiting their whole life for someone like you.

Until then, let it hurt. Let it break you if it needs to, because even that is part of your healing. When you cannot hurt anymore, you will realize that you survived it all.

Journal Prompts

1. How am I really feeling today?

_____
_____
_____
_____
_____

2. What emotions am I holding back that I need to release?

_____
_____
_____
_____

3. If I could comfort my past self, what would I say?

_____
_____
_____
_____

Day 21

Ignore the Smear Campaign!
Protect Your Peace, Not Your Name

One of the hardest parts of healing from heartbreak is accepting that your ex may try to control the narrative. Expect them to tell their version of the story, one where they are the victim and you are the villain, but that's not your battle to fight. People will judge your reaction but never question what pushed you there.

They will hear half the story and run with it because it is easier to paint you as "crazy" than to hold your ex accountable. A man will break your heart, trigger your pain, and when you finally react, he'll run off and tell everyone you lost your mind. Don't fall for it. Don't waste your energy defending yourself.

You do not need to explain your side to anyone. The people who truly know you already understand your heart. The ones who believed the lies were never in your corner to begin with. Focus on protecting your peace, not your name. Let them think whatever they want. Protect your energy. You don't owe anyone an explanation.

Healing means accepting that your side of the story no longer matters and that's okay. They won't see the wrong in their actions because they surround themselves with people who normalize them. That's not your concern. Nobody knows a man better than the woman who loved him so stand firm in what you know, and let the rest go. You are not here to convince the world. You are here to heal.

Journal Prompts

1. What emotions come up when I think about what others may have heard about me?

_____

_____

_____

_____

_____

2. How can I remind myself that my peace matters more than what others think?

_____

_____

_____

_____

_____

3. How can I practice letting go of the need to defend myself?

_____

_____

_____

_____

_____

Day 22

It's Not a Loss: It's Alignment

Sometimes, what feels like a loss is actually life aligning you with what you truly deserve. It is hard to see it when you are hurting but losing someone who didn't value you is not a loss, it is redirection. It is alignment. If someone wants to be in your life, they will make the effort. They will show up.

They will call, text, fight for the connection, and do whatever it takes to keep you. You will never have to beg, convince, or chase someone who genuinely wants you. If they don't want you in their life, there is absolutely nothing you can say or do to change their mind. Stop trying. Stop fighting for someone who has already shown you where you stand. You cannot force someone to see your worth.

Remember this: Begging someone to love you, to choose you, or to stay is not love, it's self-abandonment. You are worthy of someone who chooses you every single day without hesitation. Let this be your reminder: It wasn't a loss. It was alignment.

What left your life made space for what is meant to be. Someone who is meant for you will never put you in a position to question your value.

Journal Prompts

1. How does it feel to let go of what wasn't meant for me?

_____

_____

_____

_____

_____

2. What does alignment look like in my life and relationships moving forward?

_____

_____

_____

_____

_____

3. How can I remind myself daily that I am worthy of love that chooses me back?

_____

_____

_____

_____

_____

Day 23

You Are Enough

In the moments when you question your worth, remind yourself of everything you have already overcome the pain, the heartbreak, the nights you cried yourself to sleep. Yet, you survived it all. You are still standing, and that alone is proof of your strength. While you are busy doubting yourself, there are people who see your resilience.

There are people who need your story, your light. What you're going through right now... this heartbreak, this healing is shaping you into someone who will one day help others find their way out of the darkness. Your experience matters. Your voice matters. There is value in being an overcomer, and you are well on your way to becoming just that.

Everything you are enduring right now is equipping you with wisdom, empathy, and strength to support someone else on their journey. You are enough, exactly as you are. You do not need to prove your worth to anyone. You do not need validation from someone who could not see your value.

The right people, the ones meant for you will never make you question if you are good enough. Trust that your pain is not in vain. It is shaping you, strengthening you, and preparing you for the beautiful things ahead.

Journal Prompts

1. What are three things I've overcome that prove my strength?

_____

_____

_____

_____

_____

2. How has this experience shaped me into a more compassionate and understanding person?

_____

_____

_____

_____

_____

3. What would I say to someone else going through the same pain?

_____

_____

_____

_____

_____

Day 24

Self-Discovery and Personal Development: Finding Your Purpose

Heartbreak has a way of making you feel lost, like you've forgotten who you are outside of the relationship, but this is your chance to pause, reflect, and reconnect with yourself. This is your season of self-discovery and personal growth, the time to rediscover your purpose. Ask yourself: What do I love to do? What makes me feel truly alive? What am I passionate about?

Now is the perfect moment to revisit your interests, reignite your dreams, and embrace the things that bring you joy. Work toward becoming the healthiest, happiest, and most confident version of yourself, your best self. Explore new hobbies, step into new experiences, or rekindle old passions you once set aside. Every step forward is a step closer to what truly lights your soul.

Remember:
- It is okay to prioritize yourself and your happiness.
- Progress and joy matter more than perfection.
- Your happiness is not selfish, it is essential.
- You are allowed to make yourself a priority.

Set goals, big or small, and take steps toward them. Whether it's personal, professional, physical, or emotional growth, every effort counts. Personal development is not a destination. It is a journey. Make time to truly know yourself. Your purpose is waiting for you, and this journey you are on right now is leading you to it.

Journal Prompts

1. What are three things that bring me joy?

_____

_____

_____

_____

_____

2. What dreams or goals have I put off that I'm ready to pursue?

_____

_____

_____

_____

_____

3. How can I prioritize my happiness this week?

_____

_____

_____

_____

_____

Day 25

Set Boundaries: Not Everyone Deserves Access to You

One of the most powerful forms of self-love is learning to set boundaries. Not everyone deserves access to you, your heart, your energy, or your peace. Be protective of your space, your time, and your energy. Demand respect. Demand consistency. You have given enough of yourself to people who didn't value you. Now, it is time to choose yourself.

Setting boundaries is not about being cold or bitter; it is about honoring yourself and refusing to settle for less than you deserve. You are allowed to remove people and things from your life that no longer serve your growth, healing, or happiness. Protect your peace. Refuse to let anyone disturb your energy or control your emotions.

You are not responsible for how others choose to act, but you are responsible for how long you allow them access to your life. If protecting your peace means ending relationships, walking away, or choosing solitude for a while, do it without guilt. Choosing yourself is never the wrong decision.

Journal Prompts

1. What boundaries do I need to set to protect my peace and energy?

_____

_____

_____

_____

_____

2. Who or what in my life drains me instead of pouring into me?

_____

_____

_____

_____

_____

3. How can I practice saying no without feeling guilty?

_____

_____

_____

_____

_____

Day 26

Set Goals: Focus on Your Future

Growth begins the moment you choose to rise above your circumstances. Heartbreak may have knocked you down, but setting goals gives you something to rise toward. Your healing journey is also a time to refocus on what you truly want for yourself. What dreams have you set aside? What personal, professional, or emotional goals have you put on hold?

Now is the time to pick them back up. Make your goals a priority because you deserve to reach them. Whether it's advancing in your career, traveling, improving your health, learning something new, or simply rediscovering joy, every step forward is a reminder of your strength. Do not wait for the perfect moment.

Start small, stay consistent, and watch yourself grow. You are worthy of every dream you've ever had. Let this be your season of becoming everything you have ever imagined.

Journal Prompts

1. What are three short-term goals I can start working on today?

_____

_____

_____

_____

2. What is one long-term dream I'm ready to pursue?

_____

_____

_____

_____

_____

3. How can I hold myself accountable for my growth?

_____

_____

_____

_____

Day 27

Make a List of Reasons Why It Didn't Work

In moments of weakness, it is easy to romanticize the past and forget the reality of why the relationship ended. That's why it is important to create a list of every reason you need to heal from this breakup and let this serve as your reminder that going back is not an option. Write it all down: the red flags you ignored, the times you felt unappreciated, the moments you doubted your worth, the emotional pain you carried, and the ways you shrank yourself to be loved.

This list is not about holding onto anger or resentment; it is about grounding yourself in the truth, recognizing what didn't work for you and why you deserve better. Whenever you catch yourself missing them, fantasizing about what could have been, or feeling tempted to reach out, read your list.

Let it be your reality check. Let it remind you how far you have come and why you cannot lose yourself again by looking back. You left for a reason. Trust that reason.

Journal Prompts

1. List every reason why this relationship was not healthy for you.

_____

_____

_____

_____

_____

_____

_____

_____

_____

2. What did you compromise that you now realize you should never sacrifice again?

_____

_____

_____

_____

3. What lessons did this relationship teach you about yourself and what you need to move forward?

_____

_____

_____

Day 28

You Deserve Better

Never chase love, affection, or attention. If someone cannot offer those things freely, they are not worth your time, energy, or heart. Love should never feel like a game of convincing someone of your worth. You are worthy of someone who makes you a priority every single day. You deserve someone who chooses you, not just when it is convenient or when they're lonely, but consistently, because they recognize your value.

Be with someone who never stops flirting with you, who makes you laugh, and who is just as excited to build a future together as you are. True love does not show up with excuses; it shows up with effort.

Remember this:

- When someone truly cares, you will feel it in their actions, not just their words.
- You should never have to beg for basic love and respect.
- The right person won't have you questioning your worth or your place in their life.

Give yourself permission to move forward. Do not go back to someone who had the privilege of your love and failed to appreciate it. You have spent enough time waiting, hoping, and trying. Do not waste another moment settling for less than you deserve. When you tolerate mediocrity, you send yourself the message that it is the best you can get, but that's a lie. You deserve better. You always have.

Journal Prompts

1. Write down what you truly deserve in love and a relationship.

_____

_____

_____

_____

_____

_____

_____

_____

_____

2. What will you no longer tolerate from a partner?

_____

_____

_____

_____

_____

3. Describe the kind of love you are ready to receive moving forward.

_____

_____

_____

_____

_____

Day 29

What Did You Learn from This Experience?

We've all heard the saying: People come into your life for a reason, a season, or a lifetime. Whether it feels like it or not, every person who crosses your path teaches you something. Some lessons are painful, but all are necessary for growth. This relationship, no matter how it ended, served a purpose. Maybe it taught you how deeply you could love, how much you are willing to give, or where your boundaries need to be.

Perhaps it showed you what you will no longer tolerate or push you to finally choose yourself. There is no such thing as wasted time if you learned something. Every heartbreak, every disappointment, every moment you thought you wouldn't survive has shaped you into the stronger, wiser person you are becoming.

Ask yourself:
- *What did this experience teach me about love?*
- *What did it teach me about myself?*
- *What patterns do I need to break moving forward?*

Every lesson is guiding you toward your higher purpose - toward the life and love you truly deserve. One day, you will look back and realize this experience wasn't meant to destroy you. It was meant to awaken you.

Journal Prompts

1. Write down three lessons this breakup taught you.

_____

_____

_____

_____

_____

_____

2. What will you no longer tolerate from a partner?

_____

_____

_____

_____

_____

3. How will you use these lessons to protect your peace and guide your future relationships?

_____

_____

_____

_____

_____

Day 30

Straighten Your Crown and Remember Who You Are

You did it. You survived what you once thought would break you. Now, it is time to straighten your crown and remember exactly who you are. Your new journey requires a new mindset, new habits, and a heart ready to receive the blessings meant for you. What's ahead is far greater than what's behind.

One day, you will understand why everything had to happen the way it did. The pain had a purpose, and soon, you will reap the rewards. You are fearfully and wonderfully made. You are powerful, worthy, resilient, and strong. You have overcome so much already, and you are still standing. That alone speaks volumes about the woman you are.

Remember this:

- You cannot add days to your life, but you can add life to your days.
- Never settle for less than you deserve.
- Life is too short to be anything but happy.

When your true blessing arrives, the one sent from the Most High, you will forget what you lost. You will realize that the love you once begged for was never meant for you. What's coming is everything you have prayed for and more.

Do not give up on finding your person. Do not allow past heartbreak to dictate your future. Go where you grow and don't look back.

Every morning is a new opportunity to choose joy, to heal, and to become an even happier version of yourself. Do not start your day by carrying the broken pieces of yesterday. You have come too far to let chaos and confusion back into your life. You should never have to beg for love, attention, or effort. The right person will give it freely because it comes from the heart.

Straighten your crown, Queen. You've got this.

Healing Exercise:
Reclaiming Your Power and Self-Love

As you come to the end of this book, I want you to take a moment to reflect on your journey. Healing is not a destination. It is a continuous process of self-discovery, growth, and renewal. My hope is that by sharing my story, you have found comfort, guidance, and the reassurance that you are not alone. This exercise will help you acknowledge your progress, release lingering pain, and step fully into the empowered, healed version of yourself.

Step 1: Reflect

Find a quiet space, take a deep breath, and answer the following questions in your journal:

- What are the biggest lessons I have learned throughout my healing journey?
- How have I grown emotionally, mentally, and spiritually?
- What limiting beliefs about love and self-worth am I ready to release?

Step 2: Write a Letter to Your Past Self

Write a heartfelt letter to the version of you who was heartbroken, confused, or lost. Offer her compassion, encouragement, and wisdom from everything you have learned. Let her know that she is strong, worthy, and capable of love and happiness.

Step 3: Affirm Your Future

Write down three affirmations that resonate with the healed, empowered woman you are becoming.

Say them out loud daily:

- I am whole, worthy, and deeply loved.
- I release the past and step into my power.
- My heart is open to love, joy, and new beginnings.

Step 4: Symbolic Release

On a separate piece of paper, write down anything that no longer serves you - pain, resentment, fear, or self-doubt. Then, safely burn or tear up the paper as a symbol of letting go. Visualize yourself stepping forward with strength, confidence, and peace.

Step 5: Celebrate Yourself

Do something just for you. Take yourself on a date, buy flowers, dance to your favorite song, or spend time in nature. Celebrate how far you've come and embrace the beautiful journey ahead.

As you continue on this path, always remember:

You are powerful. You are resilient. You are love. ♡